D1530418

CLEARING THE HAZE

A Teen's Guide to Smoking-Related Health Issues

The Science of Health: Youth and Well-Being

CLEARING THE HAZE

A Teen's Guide to Smoking-Related Health Issues

by Joan Esherick

Mason Crest Publishers

Philadelphia

370 Reed Road, Broomall, Pennsylvania 19008
(866) MCP-BOOK (toll free)
www.masoncrest.com

Library of Congress Cataloging-in-Publication Data

Esherick, Joan.
  Clearing the haze: a teen's guide to smoking-related health issues/ by Joan Esherick.
     p. cm. — (The science of health)
  Includes index.
          ISBN 1-59084-844-6
          ISBN 1-59084-840-3 (series)
1. Tobacco—Toxicology. 2. Smoking—Health aspects. 3. Teenagers—Tobacco use. I. Title. II. Series.
  RA1242.T6E83 2004
  613.85—dc22
                         2004001882

First edition, 2005
13 12 11 10 09 08 07 06 05   10 9 8 7 6 5 4 3 2

Designed and produced by Harding House Publishing Service, Vestal, NY 13850.
www.hardinghousepages.com
Cover design by Benjamin Stewart.
Printed and bound in Malaysia.

This book is meant to educate and should not be used as an alternative to appropriate medical care. Its creators have made every effort to ensure that the information presented is accurate and up to date—but this book is not intended to substitute for the help and services of trained medical professionals.

CONTENTS

INTRODUCTION

by Dr. Sara Forman

You're not a little kid anymore. When you look in the mirror, you probably see a new person, someone who's taller, bigger, with a face that's starting to look more like an adult's than a child's. And the changes you're experiencing on the inside may be even more intense than the ones you see in the mirror. Your emotions are changing, your attitudes are changing, and even the way you think is changing. Your friends are probably more important to you than they used to be, and you no longer expect your parents to make all your decisions for you. You may be asking more questions and posing more challenges to the adults in your life. You might experiment with new identities—new ways of dressing, hairstyles, ways of talking—as you try to determine just who you really are. Your body is maturing sexually, giving you a whole new set of confusing and exciting feelings. Sorting out what is right and wrong for you may seem overwhelming.

Growth and development during adolescence is a multifaceted process involving every aspect of your being. It all happens so fast that it can be confusing and distressing. But this stage of your life is entirely normal. Every adult in your life made it through adolescence—and you will too.

7

But what exactly is adolescence? According to the American Heritage Dictionary, adolescence is "the period of physical and psychological development from the onset of puberty to maturity." What does this really mean?

In essence, adolescence is the time in our lives when the needs of childhood give way to the responsibilities of adulthood. According to psychologist Erik Erikson, these years are a time of separation and individuation. In other words, you are separating from your parents, becoming an individual in your own right. These are the years when you begin to make decisions on your own. You are becoming more self-reliant and less dependent on family members.

When medical professionals look at what's happening physically—what they refer to as the biological model—they define the teen years as a period of hormonal transformation toward sexual maturity, as well as a time of peak growth, second only to the growth during the months of infancy. This physical transformation from childhood to adulthood takes place under the influence of society's norms and social pressures; at the same time your body is changing, the people around you are expecting new things from you. This is what makes adolescence such a unique and challenging time.

Being a teenager in North America today is exciting yet stressful. For those who work with teens, whether by parenting them, educating them, or providing services to them, adolescence can be challenging as well. Youth are struggling with many messages from society and the media about how they should behave and who they should be. "Am I normal?" and "How do I fit in?" are often questions with which teens wrestle. They are facing decisions about their health such as how to take care of their bodies, whether to use drugs and alcohol, or whether to have sex.

This series of books on adolescents' health issues provides teens, their parents, their teachers, and all those who work with them accurate information and the tools to keep them safe and healthy. The topics include information about:

- normal growth
- social pressures
- emotional issues
- specific diseases to which adolescents are prone
- stressors facing youth today
- sexuality

The series is a dynamic set of books, which can be shared by youth and the adults who care for them. By providing this information to educate in these areas, these books will help build a foundation for readers so they can begin to work on improving the health and well-being of youth today.

1

TO SMOKE OR NOT TO SMOKE:

It's Your Choice

Would you voluntarily give up your voice for the rest of your life? Would you give away your ability to taste ice cream sundaes or smell cookies baking in the oven? Would you choose to never swim again or opt to be unable to blow out your birthday candles?

Deborah Norton wouldn't have either. But she did, unknowingly, when she chose to begin smoking cigarettes at the age of ten. She was smoking regularly by the time she reached her teens, and thirty smoking years later, doctors diagnosed her with cancer of the larynx (the voice box). To save her life, she underwent a laryngectomy (surgical removal of the voice box) and woke up after surgery without her voice.

Today, Deborah Norton breathes through a hole in the front of her neck. She has no sense of taste or smell. She makes no sound when she laughs or cries. Without a voice box, she can only speak by taking deep breaths,

Smoking is a choice—one that each individual must choose or reject for himself.

plugging the hole in her neck with her hand, and then burping the air back up from her esophagus. The sounds she makes when she forms words this way are nothing like her old voice; her words are now hoarse, raspy, and **guttural**. And she will sound this way for the rest of her life.

"No one wants to live like this out of choice," said Norton, now middle-aged, in an article put out by the American Cancer Society (www.cancer.org). "But it was a choice I made without realizing the consequences."

Smoking Is a Choice

Smoking is a choice. No one puts a gun to a nonsmoker's head and says, "Try this cigarette or I'll kill you." Most adolescents voluntarily say yes to smoking for many reasons: to be accepted by peers, to look grown-up, or because they are afraid to say no. They agree to a first cigarette, then a second, and a third, despite all the information about the hazards of smoking they've learned from parents, teachers, counselors, and law enforcement officers over the years. The truth is smoking is deadly, and teens already know that. In fact, most adolescents who begin smoking *believe* that smoking causes cancer and lung disease, but they choose to begin anyway. Why?

First, teens tend to live in the present. They think, *Smoking might hurt me someday, but it won't hurt me right now.*

Second, teens often believe they are **invincible**. They think, *Smoking might cause cancer in someone else, but it will never happen to me.*

13

Third, teens feel that smoking makes them seem more mature and independent. They think, *Smoking makes me look cool, like I'm in charge and can do what I want with my life.*

Fourth, some teens argue that smoking is enjoyable. These teens think, *I like smoking—it calms my nerves, makes me feel good, and keeps me thin.*

Let's look at each of these statements to see if they are true.

Statement #1

Smoking might hurt me someday, but it won't hurt me right now. We'll look at specific health consequences of smoking in later chapters, but consider this: most cigarettes contain about four thousand chemicals, over half of which are identified as poisons. In addition to containing nicotine, the most highly addictive substance in tobacco, cigarettes contain these toxins: arsenic (used in rat poison), carbon monoxide (same chemical found in car exhaust fumes), formaldehyde (same chemical used to preserve dead frogs intended to be dissected in science classes), hydrogen cyanide (the chemical used to kill convicted criminals sentenced to die in gas chambers), butane (used in lighter fluid), cadmium (a toxic substance found in batteries) and thousands more. Every time you hold a cigarette between your lips and inhale, you take small amounts of nicotine, formaldehyde, arsenic, and other poisons into your body. These substances don't just disappear; they enter the body and can have an almost immediate effect. Bad breath, shortness of breath, chronic coughs, gum disease, tooth decay, pneumonia, weaker lungs, and reduced physical ability in sports are only some of the short-term effects smoking can have on you right now.

14

Young people often fail to listen to adult warnings about smoking.

STATEMENT #2

Smoking might cause cancer in someone else, but it will never happen to me. Most teenagers don't think much about next month, next year, or five years from now. They tend to live for the moment, and when faced with danger or health risks they think, *It will never happen to me.* But just how invincible are teenagers, really? Consider these statistics provided by the U.S. Centers for Disease Control (CDC) and the National Childhood Cancer Foundation (NCCF): In the United States alone . . .

> between 800,000 and 900,000 teen girls get
>   pregnant each year.
> nearly 1,000 young people under age fourteen
>   drowned in 2002.

Many teens think that smoking makes them look cool.

at least one adolescent dies of an injury every
   hour of every day.
injuries kill 15,000 adolescents between the
   ages of ten and nineteen each year.
more than 4,700 sixteen- to nineteen-year-olds
   died in motor vehicle crashes in 2001.
over 12,500 young people are diagnosed with
   cancer annually.
about 2,300 children and teens die from cancer
   every year.

For an age group that thinks, *It could never happen to
me*, this list is a sobering reminder that bad stuff can and
does happen to teenagers. The kids represented by these
statistics may have thought they were invincible, but they
were wrong. It did happen to them.

STATEMENT #3

*Smoking makes me look cool, like I'm in charge and can
do what I want with my life.* So, smoking makes teens
look independent? That's exactly what the tobacco companies and advertising agencies want you to think. Tobacco companies know their products are expensive, addictive, and deadly, yet they spend billions of dollars
each year trying to get nonsmokers to become smokers.
They have to. Tobacco companies lose about five thousand customers annually, either because customers quit
smoking or they die from smoking-related diseases. The
cigarette industry would be out of business if it didn't re-
cruit new smokers to replace those it loses each year. And
where is their best place of recruitment? Teenage audiences.
   A study in the *Journal of Marketing* found that
teenagers were three times more likely to be influenced

17

by cigarette advertising than adults. Tobacco companies know this so they target teen audiences. Cartoon characters (for example, Joe Camel), free cigarette giveaways; prize **enticements** and contests, sponsorship of rock concerts and sporting events—all of these marketing ploys are designed to get teens to light up or switch brands. And, as company officials well know, once teens try smoking, they're likely to continue, and if they continue, they probably won't stop. More than 80 percent of adults who smoke regularly started smoking as teenagers.

> **Did You Know?**
>
> Tobacco use is the single most preventable cause of death in the United States each year (National Cancer Institute).

So who controls whom? Are smoking teens really independent thinkers, as they would like to believe? When tobacco companies snag teenagers as customers for life, the corporation and the drug are the ones in charge, not the teen. The company has manipulated the teen into buying its product and becoming dependent on it. The teenager's dependence on the product dictates his cravings, thoughts, and how he spends his money. He's not independent at all. Addiction isn't independence; it's slavery.

Statement #4

I like smoking—it calms my nerves, makes me feel good, and keeps me thin. Admittedly, unlike the previous three statements, there is an element of truth in this statement. Smoking does "feel good." That's true. As we'll see in the

Quitting the smoking habit is harder than starting it.

next chapter, smoking affects a part of the brain that causes pleasurable sensations. And for those addicted to nicotine, smoking can calm the agitation that comes from going without a cigarette for a period of time. But scientists have proven that nicotine is a ***stimulant*** and actually *causes* increased anxiety and nervousness.

Not only is it not an effective means to calm your nerves, but nicotine is also an ineffective weight control product. If smoking really made you thin, wouldn't all smokers be thin? Have you ever seen an overweight person smoking? Of course you have. Though smoking may reduce appetite, and may cause a *very small* amount of weight loss, it isn't a magic bullet for weight management. Smoking will not make you thin or keep you from getting fat.

Question: Which of the following kills more people each year?

car accidents
AIDS
murder
smoking
suicide
fires
alcohol
addictive drugs

Answer: If you guessed smoking, you're correct. In fact, smoking kills more people than the other seven causes of death listed combined! According to the U.S. Centers for Disease Control (CDC), one in every five deaths in the United States is smoking related. Each year, nearly a half a million Americans die from tobacco use.

Of all of these statements, none is completely true. The first three are **blatantly** false, and the fourth is only true in part. If you are going to try smoking, or if you are a smoker already, you owe it to yourself to base your decisions about smoking not on feelings or falsehood, but on truth. As cancer survivor Deborah Norton stated earlier in this chapter: *Smoking is a choice.* The rest of this book will examine the whole truth about smoking. It will give you the information you need to decide if the pleasure gained from smoking is worth the risks. We'll begin here with a few basic statements of truth.

To Smoke or Not to Smoke

True statement #1: *Tobacco use shortens your life.* According to the Palo Alto Medical Foundation, every cigarette you smoke takes away seven minutes of your life. On average, it's estimated that someone who smokes a pack or more of cigarettes each day lives seven years less that someone who never smoked. The CDC estimates that annually in the United States, premature deaths from smoking related conditions collectively rob those who have died of nearly *five million years* from what would have been their normal life spans had they not smoked. And if current trends continue, the CDC projects that five million young people (under age eighteen) who are alive today will die prematurely as adults because they chose to start smoking as adolescents.

> ### Sobering Statistics
>
> Eighty percent of adults who smoke regularly (or four out of five smokers) began smoking before the age of eighteen years. Twenty percent of these began before the age of thirteen.

True Statement #2: *Tobacco use impairs your physical fitness.* The Surgeon General's report entitled *Preventing Tobacco Use Among Young People* found that young people who smoked and participated in competitive running experienced a decline in both performance (how fast they ran) and their endurance (how long they could run). The same study found that these smokers had higher resting heart rates (meaning the heart was working too hard) and experienced far more coughs, colds, and respiratory illnesses than their nonsmoking peers. Those who started smoking as children or teens also experienced

21

stunted lung development, causing their lungs to have less capacity and function than those who never smoked.

True Statement #3: *Tobacco use is highly addictive.* Most people who smoke regularly didn't intend to when they started smoking. They only wanted to "try it once or twice" or "look cool" or "be accepted." Yet *every day* in the United States, according to the CDC, more than three thousand young people under the age of eighteen become *regular* smokers. That amounts to more than one million new young smokers each year! Nearly 90 percent of these say they wish they never started and would quit if it weren't so difficult to do so. Why is it so hard to quit? We'll discuss this in the next chapter, but this fact may give you an idea: The nicotine in tobacco is every bit as addictive as heroin and cocaine.

The Pollution of Secondhand Smoke

According to the U.S. Centers for Disease Control, secondhand smoke . . .

> fills the air with many of the same poisons found over toxic waste dumps.
> irritates eyes the way other pollutants do (redness, watering, itching).
> causes thirty times as many lung cancer deaths as other air pollutants.
> (in a crowded restaurant) can produce six times the pollution of a busy highway.
> causes 300,000 lung infections in infants and young children each year.
> kills three thousand nonsmokers each year from lung cancer alone.

True Statement #4: *Tobacco use leads to serious health problems.* In addition to causing less serious consequences like bad breath, smelly clothes, stained teeth, and wrinkled skin, tobacco use has been linked to cancer, heart disease, stroke, and lung diseases, all of which are potentially fatal. Each of these conditions will be discussed in later chapters.

Clearing the Haze

Smoking Isn't About You Alone

Yes, smoking is your choice, but it's not just about you. Smoking is a practice that also affects the health of those around you. When you smoke, you don't just inhale all the toxins discussed earlier in this chapter; you exhale them into the air around you. Not only do you exhale these poisons, but the smoke released from a lit cigarette contains toxins as well. This poisonous discharge is called second-hand smoke, and second-hand smoke kills. When a nonsmoker inhales smoke from your cigarette, she inhales the same poisons you inhale when you smoke, which puts her at risk for the very same diseases you risk contracting. The difference is that the nonsmoker isn't choosing to put herself at risk; the smoker puts her at risk.

> **Tobacco Pollution**
>
> The number one source of pollution on California beaches is cigarette butts.

"So, nonsmokers should just stay away from smokers," you might advise. True, limiting contact with smokers may help nonsmokers avoid the risks of secondhand smoke, but sometimes it's not that easy. Some places of work allow smoking; is the nonsmoker supposed to find another job? Many restaurants allow smoking, and despite attempts to create smoking and nonsmoking sections, secondhand smoke still drifts from one section to the other; is the nonsmoker supposed to stop eating out? What if an immediate family member smokes—are the

Twelve Reasons to Never Start Smoking
(or to quit if you have)

• smelly clothes, hair, car, and home
• bad breath
• wrinkled skin
• stained teeth
• heart attacks
• strokes
• cancer
• lung diseases
• reduced energy
• shortness of breath
• chronic coughs and colds
• wasted money that could have been
  spent on other things

nonsmokers in the family supposed to find a new family or move to a different house?

You might also argue, "If a person wants to commit slow suicide by smoking, that's her business; she has the right to smoke." The reality is that it isn't just her business. Secondhand smoke is an issue for everyone with whom the smoker has contact. The CDC estimates that exposure to secondhand smoke causes an estimated three thousand lung cancer deaths each year among *nonsmoking* American adults. Doesn't the nonsmoker have the right to breathe safe air?

There are other issues as well:

Who will take care of the smoker when he develops frequent colds, bronchitis, and pneumonia?

Who will pay for the smoker's hospital care or medical treatment when she develops cancer, heart problems, or lung disease?

Who will help the smoking teen catch up when he stays home sick from school?

Who will cover missed workdays when the smoker calls in sick?

Who will pay for the clean-up of increased smoking-related pollution (air pollution, butt litter, etc.)?

No, smoking isn't a choice that impacts smokers alone; it impacts everyone.

You Decide

The rest of this book deals with facts about the impact of smoking on your body, your brain, and your health. Only you can decide whether the costs of smoking (financial, physical, and emotional) are worth the pleasure it provides. Examine the facts, then make an informed decision. It's up to you.

2

TOBACCO:

What Is It, and

How Does It Affect You?

I t's been around for
centuries.

It's the most widely abused
addictive substance in
America.

It contains cyanide.

It provides a "kick" or "rush."

It's known as cigs, butts, smokes, chew, dip, snuff, and bidis.

It's an agricultural crop grown around the world.

It's a $200 billion-per-year global industry.

It contains a ***psychoactive*** ingredient that stimulates the nervous system.

It's used by more than 3.5 million American teens.

It kills someone somewhere in the world every ten seconds.

What is it?

Tobacco.

Most people have heard of tobacco. Many have seen tobacco products advertised in magazines, at concerts, or at sporting events. Tobacco products are often glamorized in films or on TV. And most know its use can be dangerous. Ninety-five percent of North American teens, some studies indicate, are aware of at least one health risk associated with tobacco. But few know exactly what tobacco does to the human body.

Tobacco: What Is It?

In order to understand how tobacco affects the human body, we first have to know what tobacco is. The product we call tobacco is a plant crop grown all over the world. It comes from several varieties of the tabacum plant, whose leaves are dried, then rolled, powdered, or crumbled, and smoked, sniffed, or chewed. Tobacco is a complex product whose smoke, when the product is burned, contains several thousand chemicals, two thousand of which are poisons, and over fifty of which cause cancer.

Tobacco

Tobacco leaves contain a highly addictive, powerful drug called nicotine. Since its identification in the early 1800s, nicotine has been studied extensively and found to affect the brain in many ways. Nicotine is the chemical in tobacco that most impacts the brain and provides the near instantaneous feelings of pleasure associated with smoking. It's what keeps smokers coming back for more.

Tobacco contains other substances as well. Tar is a thick brown sticky substance that forms when tobacco cools down. This is the substance that stains smokers' fingers and teeth and leaves a brownish residue on the

walls, drapes, curtains, and interiors of smokers' homes and cars. Tar can also collect in smokers' lungs.

Carbon monoxide, a poisonous gas (the same poison in car exhaust fumes), is a byproduct of tobacco that is released when tobacco products are burned. This gas, once inhaled, reaches the bloodstream quickly, where certain cells carry it throughout the body.

Other chemicals found in tobacco are the same chemicals found in these household products: nail polish remover (acetone), rat poison (nicotine), toilet bowl cleaner (ammonia), insecticides (DDT), and automobile batteries (cadmium). A few of these substances occur in the tobacco plant, but many are added when tobacco manufacturers process the plant to make it into various tobacco products.

The carbon monoxide produced by this traffic is the same chemical that is released when tobacco products are burned.

How Is Tobacco Used?

People have used tobacco products for centuries and have developed many ways to get tobacco into the human body. Smoking—burning the tobacco product and inhaling the smoke—is the primary way people use tobacco today. The tobacco industry produces six trillion cigarettes a year worldwide. With only six billion people living on the planet, that's enough to provide a thousand cigarettes per person per year, or nearly three cigarettes per person per day for every person in the world. That's a lot of cigarettes.

But there are other, just as potent methods of getting nicotine into the body: chewing (packing a wad of smokeless tobacco in your mouth between your gum and cheek) and snuffing (inhaling powdered tobacco into your nose) are two less popular, but still common, methods.

Tobacco and the Brain

Nicotine, the primary psychoactive (brain-acting) ingredient of tobacco, enters the body through the skin, lungs, or mucous membranes (that is, the lining of your nose, mouth, or gums). Inhaling cigarette smoke delivers nicotine to the lungs. Your lungs contain millions of small air sacs called alveoli where, during a regular breath, oxygen from the air is exchanged for carbon dioxide, which you exhale. When you smoke, nicotine enters the air sacs the same way oxygen does and from there moves into your bloodstream. It flows almost immediately to your brain, and then on to the rest of your body.

Most cigarettes in the United States today contain ten to twenty milligrams of nicotine per cigarette. The average smoker inhales only about one to two milligrams of that nicotine, yet this small amount has a large effect. Inhaled nicotine travels through the lungs, into the bloodstream, and to the brain within ten seconds, sometimes reaching the brain in as little as eight seconds after taking a puff.

Cigar and pipe smokers don't usually inhale smoke the way cigarette smokers do, so they deliver nicotine to their bodies primarily through the mucous membranes of their mouths and noses. Chewing tobacco never enters the lungs; it, too, is absorbed through the mouth's membranes. In both cases, nicotine is absorbed through the membrane and directly into the bloodstream where it is delivered to other parts of the body.

Once in the brain, nicotine affects communication between special nerve cells in the brain, called neurons. Neurons are responsible for receiving and transmitting messages from other neurons, but they can't do the job alone. They use chemical messengers known as neurotransmitters to carry these messages from neuron to neuron within the brain. Nicotine acts on a specific type of neurotransmitter called acetylcholine, which delivers signals from your brain to your muscles, controls your energy level, controls how fast your heart beats and how often you take a breath, oversees the flow of information throughout your brain (how fast and how slow messages are transmitted between neurons), and enables you to learn and remember things.

Nicotine increases the amount of acetylcholine in the brain, which increases the amount of messages being transmitted between brain cells. This causes an almost immediate feeling of alertness in the smoker, a rise in energy level, and what seems like an increased ability to pay attention or focus.

Nicotine also increases how much of a second neurotransmitter, called dopamine, is released in the brain. Dopamine works in the part of your brain responsible for survival instincts (eating, reproduction, etc.), happy feelings, and pleasurable sensations. It is sometimes called "the pleasure molecule." It is the same neurotransmitter affected by highly addictive drugs like

> **Did You Know?**
>
> Nicotine inhaled through cigarettes or cigars takes only seconds to reach the brain, but has a direct effect on the body for up to thirty minutes.

One reason that smoking is so addictive is that lighting up gives smokers a "pleasure rush."

heroin and cocaine. An increase in dopamine is what many smokers experience as peaceful, pleasurable, calm feelings. Dopamine levels are also considered the root of most chemical addictions.

In addition to neurotransmitters, nicotine can cause your brain to increase production of endorphins, your body's pain-killing proteins. These natural analgesics (painkillers) can cause feelings of *euphoria*—like a runner's high—and reduce awareness of pain. More pleasure; less pain—no wonder people enjoy smoking!

The downside of nicotine is that its effect on the brain doesn't last. The brain cries out for more nicotine as soon

According to medical research, teen smokers are more prone to various anxiety disorders.

as thirty minutes after finishing a cigarette. That's why many teen smokers admit to feeling nicotine cravings even after trying only one or two cigarettes. The good feelings nicotine supplies are short-lived, requiring the tobacco user to use tobacco products more and more.

Another downside of nicotine is that some of the neurotransmitters responsible for nicotine's energetic feelings or short-term highs are the same neurotransmitters involved in **anxiety disorders** and depression. A recent study published in the *Journal of the American Medical Association* found that teen smokers became more prone to generalized anxiety disorders, panic attacks, and agoraphobia (fear of public places) than their nonsmoking peers. In another article, the American Psychological Association, quoting a study published in *Pediatrics* magazine, reported that smoking was the single strongest predictor of a teen's developing depressive symptoms. Among nondepressed teens, those who smoked were four times more likely to develop depression than those who did not. Why? Because of nicotine's impact on the brain.

Nicotine changes brain chemistry. Think about it. On average, a smoker will take ten puffs on one cigarette over about five minutes. A person who smokes thirty cigarettes a day (a pack and a half), then, gets three hundred jolts of nicotine per day. Over time, your brain chemistry changes so that your brain expects the nicotine jolt and compensates for nicotine's effects in such a way that you need more and more nicotine to create the desired effect. Your brain gets used to having nicotine, so if you try to stop smoking, your brain can't function like it did without it (at least until it gets used to not having nicotine again). This dependence on nicotine is called addiction.

Tobacco and the Body

Inhaled nicotine, the addictive chemical in tobacco, doesn't only impact the brain; it works on other areas of the body. At first, nicotine causes your body to release a hormone called adrenaline—the same hormone that is triggered by fear. Most of us have experienced an "adrenaline rush" when riding a particularly frightening roller coaster, when terrified by a scary movie, or when nearly being involved in a traffic accident. Adrenaline causes your heart to beat faster, your breathing rate to increase, and your blood pressure to rise. Nicotine has the same effect.

While it's causing a release of adrenaline, inhaled nicotine simultaneously blocks the release of another hormone called insulin. Too little insulin results in higher levels of sugar in your blood—a condition called hyperglycemia—so that your body cuts back on its demand for food. This causes the reduced appetite many smokers experience.

Nicotine, remember, is a poison. It's been used as a pesticide (to kill insects on plants) for hundreds of years. If eaten, not inhaled, it causes vomiting, nausea, headaches, breathing difficulties, stomach pain, and **seizures**. It takes only 60 milligrams of ingested nicotine (the amount contained in three or four cigarettes) to kill an adult. Thousands of small children end up in emergency rooms all over North America each year because they ingest their parents' cigarettes or eat cigarette butts from their parents' ashtrays.

In addition to nicotine, other chemicals from tobacco travel throughout the body, impacting organs and tissues in a variety of ways. The specifics of these sometimes fatal effects will be discussed in the next two chapters, but for now it's important to realize that these effects are serious enough for governments all over the world to require warnings on tobacco product packages (see sidebars).

Cigarette Package Warnings
in the United States

1966 through 1970:
"CAUTION: CIGARETTE SMOKING MAY BE HAZARDOUS TO YOUR HEALTH"

1970 through 1985:
"WARNING: THE SURGEON GENERAL HAS DETERMINED THAT CIGARETTE SMOKING IS DANGEROUS TO YOUR HEALTH."

Since 1985 these four warnings have had to appear on cigarette packages (rotating quarterly):
"SURGEON GENERAL'S WARNING: Smoking Causes Lung Cancer, Heart Disease, Emphysema, and May Complicate Pregnancy."
"SURGEON GENERAL'S WARNING: Quitting Smoking Now Greatly Reduces Serious Risks to Your Health."
"SURGEON GENERAL'S WARNING: Smoking by Pregnant Women May Result in Fetal Injury, Premature Birth and Low Birth Weight."
"SURGEON GENERAL'S WARNING: Cigarette Smoking Contains Carbon Monoxide."

Cigarette Package Warnings in Canada

Sixteen different health-warning messages appear on Canadian tobacco product packages. Some of these messages include graphic photographs of oral cancer, diseased lungs, and in-your-face statements including:

"Tobacco products are highly addictive."
"Your chances of surviving [lung cancer] are low. Eighty percent of lung cancer victims die within one year."
"Tobacco use triples the risk of heart disease."
"Smoking during pregnancy can harm your baby."

Knowledge of tobacco's composition and how it affects the brain and body isn't the only information you need to make a wise choice about using tobacco. You need to know about tobacco products, as well.

Smokeless Tobacco Product Package Warnings in the United States

"WARNING: This product may cause mouth cancer."
"WARNING: This product may cause gum disease and tooth loss."
"WARNING: This product is not a safe alternative to cigarettes."

Cigar Package Warnings in the United States

"SURGEON GENERAL'S WARNING: Cigar Smoking Can Cause Cancers of the Mouth and Throat, Even If You Do Not Inhale."
"SURGEON GENERAL'S WARNING: Cigar Smoking Can Cause Lung Cancer and Heart Disease."
"SURGEON GENERAL'S WARNING: Tobacco Use Increases the Risk of Infertility, Stillbirth and Low Birth Weight."
"SURGEON GENERAL'S WARNING: Cigars Are Not a Safe Alternative to Cigarettes."
"SURGEON GENERAL'S WARNING: Tobacco Smoke Increases the Risk of Lung Cancer and Heart Disease, Even in Non-smokers."

Each cigarette package is required by law to have a warning.

Warnings on Other Tobacco Product Labels in Canada

Bidis:
"USE OF THIS PRODUCT CAN CAUSE CANCER"
"TOBACCO SMOKE HURTS CHILDREN"
"TOBACCO SMOKE CAN CAUSE FATAL LUNG DISEASES"
"TOBACCO SMOKE CONTAINS HYDROGEN CYANIDE"

Chewing tobacco and oral snuff:
"THIS PRODUCT IS HIGHLY ADDICTIVE"
"THIS PRODUCT CAUSES MOUTH DISEASES"
"THIS PRODUCT IS NOT A SAFE ALTERNATIVE TO CIGARETTES"
"USE OF THIS PRODUCT CAN CAUSE CANCER"

Nasal snuff:
"THIS PRODUCT IS NOT A SAFE ALTERNATIVE TO CIGARETTES"
"THIS PRODUCT CONTAINS CANCER CAUSING AGENTS"
"THIS PRODUCT MAY BE ADDICTIVE"
"THIS PRODUCT MAY BE HARMFUL"

Warning on Cigarette Package
Labels in France

"SMOKING KILLS."

Facts About Tobacco Products in the United States

Tobacco products come in many shapes and sizes. Cigarettes, cigars, and pipes are the products with which you are probably most familiar. And you've probably heard of "smokeless tobacco" products, like chewing tobacco that was so popular among baseball players in the twentieth century and that has become popular among teens today. But in recent years, new varieties of cigarettes and smokeless tobacco have entered the market claiming to be "safe" alternatives.

Recent marketing trends tout these tobacco products as more natural and safer than conventional cigarettes: "low tar" and "low nicotine" cigarettes; "unfiltered, additive-free" cigarettes (no chemical additives of preservatives); flavored smokeless chews (e.g.: Cherry Skoal); clove cigarettes (also called kreteks, which contain 30 to 40 percent ground cloves); and bidis (pronounced "beedies," which are small cigarettes flavored to taste like candy). The popularity of these "alternatives" among teens has grown rapidly in recent years and continues to rise. Teens view them as "safe."

But, frankly, there is no such thing as a "safe" cigarette.

Bidis, known as "the poor man's cigarette," are imported from India. They come rolled in an unprocessed tobacco leaf tied with strings and look a lot like a marijuana joint. They are cheaper to buy than commercial cigarettes and easier for young people to obtain. Though bidis may be smaller and contain less tobacco per cigarette, they are unfiltered and contain higher concentrations of nicotine, tar, and carbon monoxide. In other words, though they have less tobacco per product than cigarettes, bidis provide more poison. Despite their appealing flavors (chocolate, strawberry, vanilla, licorice, and mango), bidis are more addictive, and every bit as harmful as, old-fashioned cigarettes.

> The average first-time smokeless tobacco user is ten years old.

Clove cigarettes come from Indonesia and contain a mix of roughly 70 percent tobacco and 30 percent ground cloves (can be a ratio of sixty-forty). The tobacco used in a clove cigarette is the very same tobacco used in a conventional cigarette and carries the very same health risks. And it's every bit as addictive.

Additive-free cigarettes may not have any chemical additives or preservatives added in production, but they still contain tobacco. In fact, when testing various types

Tobacco plants.

of cigarettes, the U.S. National Institute on Drug Abuse found that additive-free cigarettes raised nicotine levels in smokers' bloodstreams higher than any other type of cigarette.

"Low tar" and "low nicotine" cigarettes, also known as "light" or "ultra light" cigarettes, claim to have lower cancer risks. According to the CDC, however, cigarettes with lower tar and nicotine contents are not substantially less hazardous to your health than higher content brands. Smokers who switch to these brands often change their smoking habits—puffing more, inhaling more deeply, smoking more often—to make up for the reduced effects of less nicotine per cigarette, and end up consuming as many toxins, if not more, than had they stayed with regular brands.

> "Smoking low tar and nicotine cigarettes is the equivalent of jumping out of the twenty-ninth floor of a building rather than the thirty-first."
>
> —Kenneth Warner and John Slades in *The American Journal of Public Health*, January 1992

Smokeless tobacco, also known as "chewing tobacco," "spit tobacco," or "chew," is perhaps the most widely misunderstood form of tobacco. A study conducted by the U.S. Department of Health and Human Services found that six out of ten junior high users and four out of ten senior high users thought that regular spit tobacco use carried little or no health risks. They couldn't be more wrong. Though it is not inhaled, smokeless tobacco comes in direct contact with the membranes of the mouth and gum, and it contains just as much nicotine. The chemicals found in smokeless tobacco are the very same chemicals found in inhaled forms of tobacco, and once they pass through the mouth's mucous membranes, they travel through the body in much the same way. Smokeless tobacco is no safer than its inhaled counterpart.

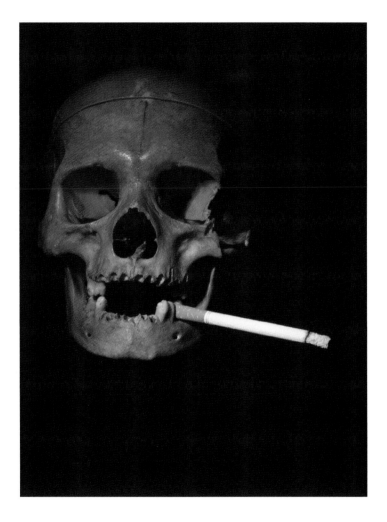

Smoking kills!

A Caution from the CDC

WARNING: There is no safe tobacco product. The use of any tobacco product can cause cancer and other adverse health effects. This includes all forms of tobacco including cigarettes, cigars, pipes, and spit tobacco; ***mentholated***, "low-tar," "naturally grown," or "additive free."

In this chapter, we've learned about tobacco: what it is, how it enters the body, how it impacts the brain, and how it initially impacts us physically. We've also learned about several so-called alternative tobacco products that claim to be "safe" but are not. If there is no such thing as a "safe" cigarette, what are the dangers? We'll take a look at these in detail next.

3

TOBACCO'S BIG RISK:

Cancer

I *didn't know it was bad for me. I mean, I saw all these guys on Major League benches with wads in their cheeks. If pro ball players chewed spit tobacco, then it must not be bad for you, right? I just wanted to do what other ball players did, so I started chewing snuff when I was thirteen. By the time I reached high school, I was dipping about three cans a week, and didn't think anything of it. I still ran three or four miles a day; I was the starting first-baseman on the varsity baseball team; I medaled in winter track. I was even offered an athletic scholarship. Everything was great. Then I got this sore in my mouth that wouldn't go away.*

I couldn't believe it when the doctor said it was cancer— **squamous cell carcinoma** *was the fancy term he used. Cancer? I'm only eighteen! This doesn't happen to people like me—not athletes, not guys who work out and take fitness seriously. I exercise, I eat right, I don't smoke or drink or do drugs. I take care of myself. I just dipped out of habit. Now the docs say they have to take out half of my tongue, the jaw bone on one side of my mouth, and the neck muscles and glands on that side of my head. When they're done with surgery, I won't have a face left. And I won't be able to talk anymore. So much for college. So much for baseball. I'll be lucky if I live.*

I was only ten years old when I saw the movie Grease *for the first time. I thought Olivia Newton John was so pretty and, man, could she sing! When her character in the movie decided that being "good" like Sandra Dee wouldn't attract boys, I agreed. So I started smoking, just like she did. I thought it made me look cool and grown-up, even glamorous.*

I had no idea that twelve years later, when I graduated from college and was ready to move out on my own, I'd be facing lung cancer. There I was: twenty-two years old, back home again, coughing my lungs out, and living with Mom and Dad. I could barely go up steps without running out of breath. Sometimes at night, I woke up coughing and gasping for air. Sometimes I just felt like I was suffocating.

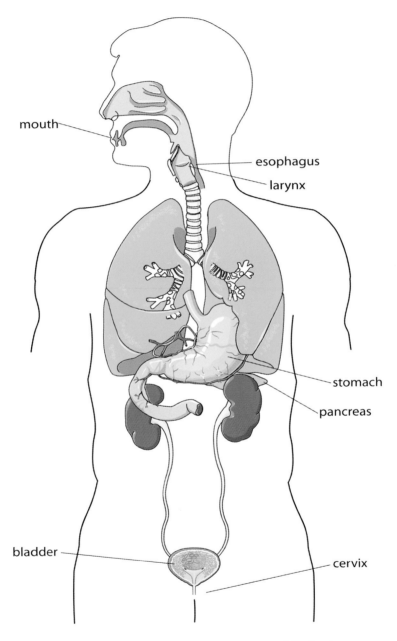

mouth

esophagus

larynx

stomach

pancreas

bladder

cervix

Smoking can cause cancer in many areas of the body.

Tobacco's Big Risk: Cancer

They never show you this side of smoking in the movies—the gross phlegm that you cough out of your lungs, the bloody Kleenex, the inability to breathe. It's all glamour and no truth. I wish I had known.

*I had **leukemia** when I was little. My parent's told me I was two years old when they found out. I don't remember much about that now. I just know I got better. I'm a cancer survivor. But even that wasn't enough to keep me from smoking. All my friends smoked, my parents smoked, it seemed like everybody I saw in the movies smoked. So I did, too. When I was about twelve, I started taking drags off friends' cigarettes, just to be included. I liked it. Then I started buying my own packs, like in vending machines at the bowling alley. I'm up to about a pack a day now, but don't nag me. Yeah, I cough more, and I get a lot of colds, and I can't run like I used to, but I like smoking. It makes me feel good. So back off. I KNOW smoking causes cancer, but I figure that if I beat cancer once, I can beat it again.*

These three fictional accounts represent real people who made the choice to use tobacco products. Two regretted the choice; one stayed in denial. But each knew what tobacco was and what cancer could do. They illustrate some of the risks associated with tobacco use.

One of the greatest risks tobacco users face is the development of cancer. While much mystery about cancer remains,

> **Did You Know?**
>
> Cancers are usually named for the organ in which they originate. A cancer that begins in the lungs is called lung cancer. A cancer that begins on the skin is called skin cancer.

doctors and scientists have long known about the link between tobacco use and increased incidence of various types of cancers in tobacco users.

The Big Risk: Cancer

The eighteen-year-old track star who opened this chapter contracted one kind of cancer. The twenty-two-year-old who followed contracted another. Cancer comes in many forms.

When we hear the term "cancer" we often think of one disease. In reality, the word refers to several different diseases that share certain things in common. The American Cancer Society describes cancer this way:

> Cancer develops when cells in a part of the body begin to grow out of control. Although there are many kinds of cancer, they all start because of out-of-control growth of abnormal cells. . . . Because cancer cells continue to grow and divide, they are different from normal cells. Instead of dying, they outlive normal cells and continue to form new abnormal cells.
>
> Cancer cells develop because of damage to **DNA**. . . . People can inherit damaged DNA, which accounts for inherited cancers. Many times though, a person's DNA becomes damaged by exposure to something in the environment, like smoking.

Tobacco-related cancers can occur nearly anywhere in the body's major systems, but they tend to occur more frequently in those areas that have direct contact with tobacco's chemicals. The most common tobacco-related cancers occur in the mouth, throat, and lungs.

> ### Types of Cancer Linked to Tobacco Use
>
> - lung cancer
> - cancers of the mouth and throat (oral, esophageal, laryngeal)
> - bladder cancer
> - kidney cancer
> - pancreatic cancer
> - cervical cancer

Cancers of the Mouth

Cancers of the mouth, also known as oral cancers, are particularly brutal. According to the Oral Cancer Foundation (www.oralcancerfoundation.org), over 30,000 Americans are diagnosed with oral or pharyngeal (cancers of the pharynx, which is located between the mouth and the esophagus) cancers each year. Less than half of these will still be alive five years after their diagnoses. Oral cancer kills one person every hour, twenty-four hours a day, every year. Seventy-five percent of these, or three out of four, are tobacco users.

In its earliest stages, oral cancer can look like less serious conditions. It can show up as a white or red spot on your tongue, under your tongue, or the inside of your cheek. It might look like an acid pimple, a common canker sore, or a cold sore on your lips. Sometimes it will appear as a solid lump that you can feel inside your mouth, tongue, or neck. It can also seem like a bad case of laryngitis, a hoarseness that just won't quit. Other times, the first symptoms may be pain, numbness, or difficulty when you swallow, talk, or eat. In later stages, it can look like a bumpy wart at the very back of your mouth, either on your tongue or near your tonsils.

The treatment of oral cancer usually involves some combination of surgery, radiation therapy (where cancer cells are **bombarded** with high doses of radiation in an effort to kill them), and chemotherapy (where cancer

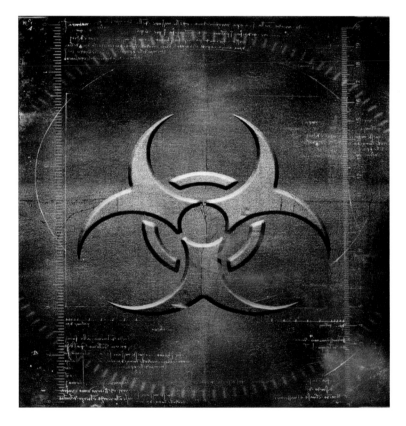

Tobacco products are hazardous materials.

Cigarette smoking causes at least 30 percent of all cancer deaths. It causes 87 percent of lung cancer deaths, and over 90 percent of oral (mouth) and laryngeal (voice box) cancers.

cells are "poisoned" with certain chemicals in an attempt to kill them). Surgical treatment for oral cancer is almost always necessary and is often disfiguring. Imagine what you would look like without your jawbone or neck muscles. Imagine how difficult it would be to eat if you only had half of your tongue. Yet these sacrifices are what keep oral cancer patients alive.

Oral cancer is a high price to pay for the short-lasting pleasure chewing tobacco or cigarettes provide. Would you agree?

Cancers of the Throat

If tobacco can cause cancer in the mouth, it's not difficult to see how it might cause cancer of the throat. Tobacco smokers, sniffers, and chewers all put their throats in direct contact with the tobacco products they use.

Two parts of the throat are most commonly affected by the chemicals in tobacco: the esophagus (the tube that runs

Did You Know?

Each year cancer kills more young people under twenty years of age than asthma, diabetes, AIDS, and cystic fibrosis combined!

57

Real People, Real Cancer, Real Lives

Read these on-line stories of people who faced tobacco-related cancers:

- nineteen-year-old former track star Sean Marsee (now deceased)
  http://whyquit.com/whyquit/SeanMarsee.html

- twenty-five-year-old oral cancer survivor Gruen Von Behrens
  http://www.nstep.org/

---

from the back of the mouth to the stomach) and the larynx (the voice box). Cancer can develop in both: esophageal cancer is cancer of the esophagus, and laryngeal cancer is cancer of the larynx.

The National Cancer Institute estimates that over 10,000 people are diagnosed with laryngeal cancer per year, or nearly thirty people per day. The American Cancer Society estimates that in the same time period over 14,000 new cases of esophageal cancers will be diagnosed, or thirty-five people per day. And that's just in the United States. Other countries, like China, Iran, India, and southern parts of Africa where smoking is far more prevalent and acceptable, have ten to one hundred times the rate of esophageal cancer cases per year than the United States.

Tobacco's Big Risk: Cancer

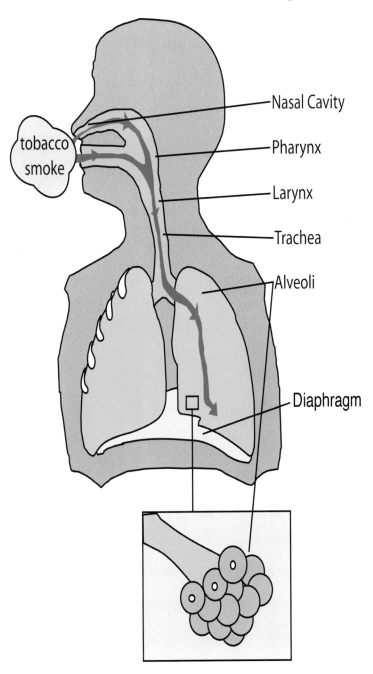

tobacco smoke

Nasal Cavity

Pharynx

Larynx

Trachea

Alveoli

Diaphragm

Clearing the Haze

One of the most difficult aspects of laryngeal cancer for patients to deal with (apart from the threat of death) is having their larynx removed as part of their treatment. The larynx contains the vocal cords, which give sound to

Celebrities Who Died From Tobacco-Related Cancers

- Babe Ruth (baseball player), of throat cancer at age 53
- Carl Wilson (of the Beach Boys), of lung cancer at age 51
- Michael Landon (actor), of pancreatic cancer at age 54
- Walt Disney, of lung cancer at age 65
- Carrie Hamilton (actress Carol Burnett's daughter), of lung cancer at age 38
- Sammy Davis, Jr. (singer/entertainer), of throat cancer at age 64
- Nat "King" Cole (musician), of lung cancer at age 45
- Luiz Jose Costa (Brazilian music star), of lung cancer at age 36
- Eric Carr (drummer for KISS), of lung cancer at age 41
- Graham Chapman (of Monty Python), of throat cancer at age 48
- Humphrey Bogart (actor), of esophageal cancer at age 57
- Sigmund Freud (psychoanalyst), of oral cancer at age 83

> **Smoking Is a Radiating Experience!**
>
> Smoking a pack and a half of cigarettes per day for a year exposes the lining of the lungs to the same amount of radiation (from the lead in tobacco leaves) as would be found in having 1,600 chest X rays.

your voice. Without vocal cords, you lose your ability to talk as you once did. Patients who have their voice boxes removed have to learn to talk again in a different way. They never sound the same again. These patients also lose much of their sense of taste and smell—another huge loss, especially if you enjoy eating.

The sad thing about cancers of the throat is that many can be prevented. Over 90 percent of laryngeal cancers are caused by smoking tobacco products! Limiting contact with tobacco products greatly reduces your risk of developing either of these deadly diseases.

Lung Cancer

Though using tobacco products can cause many types of cancer, including mouth and throat cancers, lung cancer is the cancer most commonly associated with smoking. It makes up almost one-fourth of all cancer deaths. That means that one out of every four people who die from cancer (counting all types) dies from lung cancer.

It's a known fact that nearly 90 percent of all lung cancers are caused by smoking. But we've heard that figure so often that it's become a statistic we largely ignore. Let's try a different approach.

Think of it this way: if you knew that in forty years an awful *plague* was going to come and wipe out over 160,000 people your age, and you had a secret formula that would keep nearly 140,000 of them alive, wouldn't you do something to save them? Wouldn't you give the formula to as many people as you could? Wouldn't you take the formula yourself to keep from dying?

Lung cancer is most often diagnosed in people between the ages of fifty-five and seventy—today's teenagers in roughly forty years. The American Cancer Society estimates that lung cancer will kill 160,000 adults each year. Seven out of eight of these deaths are entirely preventable. Nearly 140,000 of these adults can be saved.

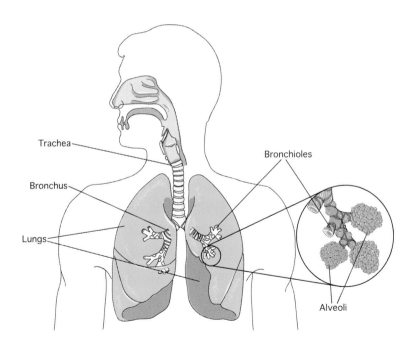

Clearing the Haze

What is the formula? It's simple: don't use tobacco products. If all the people predicted to die from future lung cancer deaths caused by smoking chose not to smoke, over 140,000 lives could be saved per year.

Lung cancer provides a cruel, slow, painful death. There's nothing noble or glamorous about it. Coughing, spitting up blood, gasping for air, extreme weakness, the need to be hooked up to an oxygen machine—this is what lung cancer patients have to look forward to.

This kind of cancer begins in the lungs. The right lung has three sections, called lobes. The left lung, which allows room for the heart, only has two. The lungs are what enable us to inhale and exhale and move air in and out of our bodies. When we inhale, we take in good air, which contains needed oxygen, and when we exhale, we get rid of bad air, a waste product called carbon dioxide.

For air to get into our bodies, it must travel down the windpipe into the lungs. The single windpipe divides into two tubes called bronchi (forming a kind of upside-down "Y"), each of which leads to a lung. Once in the lung, the bronchi divide into smaller branches called bronchioles, in the same way that tree branches divide and get smaller as you go further out the limbs. At the end of these small branches are tiny air sacs called alveoli. It's in these air sacs, kind of like leaves on a tree, where our bodies exchange carbon dioxide (the bad air we exhale) for oxygen (that we inhale).

Most lung cancers affect the bronchi first, but they can also start in other places such as the **trachea**, bronchioles, or alveoli. Wherever it starts invading healthy respiratory tissue cells with the uncontrolled growth of cancer's abnormal cells, lung cancer makes it progressively harder to breathe and get the oxygen the body needs. Death from lung cancer is often like long, slow suffocation that can take months or even years.

Treatments for lung cancer vary depending on the type of lung cancer, its severity, and when it is diagnosed. Like other cancers, most lung cancers are treated with a combination of surgery (to remove the cancerous part of the lungs), radiation therapy, and chemotherapy. Despite these efforts, most people do not survive lung cancer. Of those who are diagnosed with lung cancer, only 40 percent (only two out of five) will still be alive a year later. And only one out of ten (roughly 13 percent) will be alive five years after they are diagnosed.

Sadly, if statistics are accurate, the three people whose stories opened this chapter will die early, unnecessary deaths from entirely preventable cancers. Some will die young, as our eighteen-year-old baseball player with oral cancer eventually did; others may not die until they are much older. In the end, however, cancer will kill all of them. All they needed to do was not smoke or not chew, and they might have remained cancer-free. The choice was theirs.

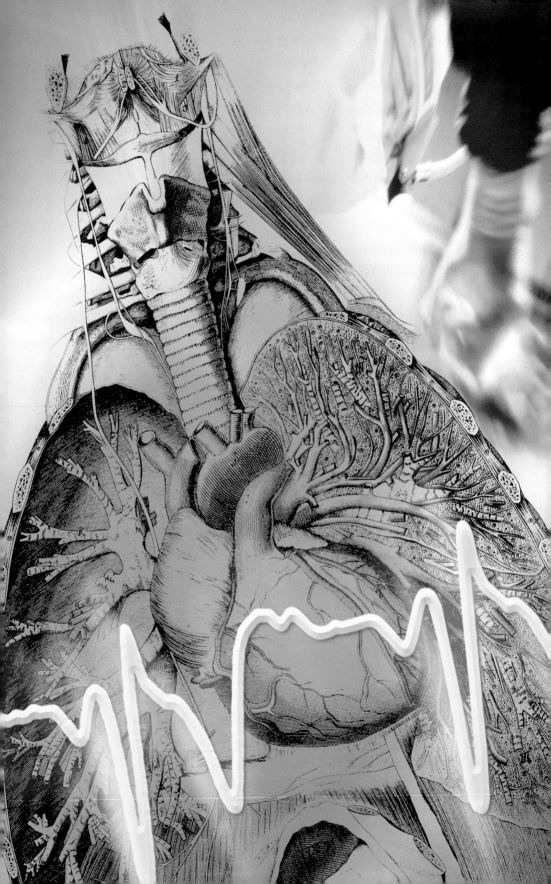

4

More Big Risks:

Heart Disease, Stroke, and Lung Disorders

Amanda (age twenty-three): *I've been smoking since I was fifteen, but not a lot—only about a pack a week. I am starting to have breathing* *problems and sometimes I wake up in the middle of the night gasping for air. It scares me. I used to like to run track, but I can't do that anymore. Now I'm happy if I can manage to walk a mile or two without coughing the whole way home. What's happening to me?*

Scott (age twenty-nine): *I started smoking when I was twelve. I have **emphysema** now and am on three liters of oxygen 24/7. I walk around with a tube in my nose, **tethered** to an oxygen machine so I can breathe, but, believe it or not, I still smoke; I just turn the oxygen off when I smoke so it won't blow up. I want to quit, though. I've tried to quit before, but I just couldn't, even though I know the smokes are killing me. I wish I'd never seen a cigarette.*

Jolene (age fourteen): *I'm a nonsmoker who was brought up in a smoking family. I've had **asthma** all my life. Then I got pneumonia, went to the ER, and found out I had chronic **bronchitis**, in addition to my asthma. I've had shortness of breath and frequent asthma attacks ever since. And I never even tried a cigarette. Not even once. It's not fair. How come they get to smoke, and I get to pay?*

Angel (age seventeen): *I was diagnosed with **upper respiratory failure** when I was eleven. I kept wheezing and never could seem to get enough breath. I felt like someone was always pressing on my chest. A few years later, another doctor told me that I didn't have respiratory failure at all, but that I had chronic bronchitis. He put me on inhalers to control my condition but it only got worse. Recently, a lung specialist told me that it's not either of those things. Instead, he said I have emphysema. I do not smoke, but my parents do. Their secondhand smoke caused my lung conditions. I try as hard as I can to live with my lung*

68

disease but it's hard. Sometimes I'm afraid, but I believe in never giving up!

Katie (age twenty-one): *I promised myself I would quit smoking when I finished finals, so when the semester ended, I threw out my last carton of cigarettes and quit cold turkey. Soon after, I went to the grocery store to buy some lollypops—they helped me not want to put a ciga-rette in my mouth—and when I went to pay the cashier I experienced a pain in my head so severe I thought my head would explode. I grabbed the lady behind me and told her to call 911. Something was really wrong. The last thing I remember was falling to the floor.*

*I later found out that I had an **intracerebral hemor-rhage**—what some people call a bleeding stroke, and I was only twenty-one. Thankfully doctors were able to op-erate on my brain quickly enough to prevent severe brain damage, but I now have seizures. I also have trouble with my right side. But I'm thankful to be alive. They tell me that they don't really know why I had the stroke, but that smoking probably increased my chances of having it.*

Jamal (age fifteen): *I was running on the basketball court, shooting hoops with the team, when all of a sudden I felt like someone was standing on my chest. I couldn't breathe. I started sweating a bunch. And I couldn't move my left arm. Coach called 911. The ambulance took me to the hospital. I had to stay a few days. They said I had a heart attack. A heart attack! At fifteen! Heart attacks only hap-pen to old people. Why me? Sure, I liked cigs, and was al-ways passing butts with my friends, but never thought they'd make me sick. The docs aren't exactly sure what happened, but they said smoking only makes it more likely to happen again. I haven't touched a butt since.*

69

Clearing the Haze

We saw in the last chapter that tobacco use leads to several different types of cancer—a fact with which most people are familiar. The quotes that open this chapter, however, reveal another dark side of tobacco use: its link to heart disease, strokes, and chronic lung disease.

Take a look at these statistics:

- Eighty to 90 percent of people with chronic obstructive pulmonary disease (COPD)—a group of lung diseases—have a history of significant tobacco use.
- The CDC estimates that men and women who smoke are ten times more likely to die of bronchitis and emphysema than those who stay smoke-free.
- The U.S. Department of Health and Human Services affirms that the risk of stroke in people who smoke is 50 percent higher than those who do not.
- The CDC also estimates that tobacco use *triples* your risk of dying from heart disease and doubles your risk of sudden cardiac death (heart attack).
- The U.S. Surgeon General views cigarette smoking as so dangerous to heart health, in fact, that he calls it "the most important of the modifiable risk factors for coronary heart disease in the United States."

Tobacco use almost always leads to health trouble, as Amanda, Scott, Jolene, Angel, Katie, and Jamal can testify.

71

Clearing the Haze

> ### Major Risk Factors for CAD
>
> - smoking
> - physical inactivity
> - excess weight
> - high blood pressure
> - high cholesterol
> - stress

Tobacco and Heart Disease

Fifteen-year-old Jamal had a sudden, unpredictable heart attack. Heart attack happens when the heart muscle's supply of blood and oxygen is cut off, usually because of one of several different heart diseases. Coronary artery disease (CAD) is the most common heart disease that causes heart attacks.

CAD causes the coronary arteries, the big, tube-like blood vessels that carry oxygen-rich blood to the heart,

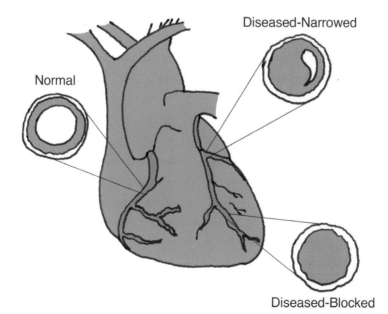

Normal

Diseased-Narrowed

Diseased-Blocked

to become clogged. Sometimes a substance called *plaque* builds up along the inside walls of the arteries making them narrower and less flexible. It would be like caking the inside of a garden hose with layers of glue that harden and gradually close off the hose until no more water can seep through. As years go by, the build up of plaque can limit the amount of blood that reaches the heart, cut off the supply of blood to the heart completely, or cause the blood to clot (when blood cells clump together and harden) and block the artery.

> **Did You Know?**
>
> Most people with hypertension (high blood pressure) feel just fine. That's why hypertension is sometimes called the "silent killer."

Smoking tobacco products contributes to CAD several ways. First, it affects the production of a substance in the body called cholesterol. There are two kinds of cholesterol: a good kind (called HDL) and a bad kind (called LDL). HDL is considered good because it seems to protect against heart attack. LDL is considered bad because too much of it can increase the build up of plaque in the coronary arteries, making it easier for them to become blocked. Smoking increases the production of LDL and decreases the production of HDL.

Smoking also increases the tendency of blood to clot, making it more likely that blood clots might form in the arteries and block blood flow to the heart. It also increases blood pressure. (Blood pressure is simply the measure of how hard your blood pushes against your veins and arteries as it flows through them.) High blood pressure can cause your arteries to harden with plaque faster, making a heart attack or stroke more likely. It can also cause a vessel to rupture.

Signs of a Stroke

- sudden, unexplained severe headache
- sudden difficulty walking or loss of balance
- sudden numbness or weakness on one side of the body (can be in the face, arm, or leg)
- sudden mental confusion
- sudden difficulty with speaking or understanding speech
- sudden trouble seeing in one or both eyes

Smoking contributes to other heart conditions as well: atherosclerosis ("hardening of the arteries"); arrhythmias (a change in the regular beat of the heart); and angina (chest pain), among others. But smoking doesn't only affect blood flow in and around the heart; it can also affect blood flow to the brain.

TOBACCO AND STROKE

Twenty-one-year-old Katie learned firsthand what it was like to have a stroke. She was lucky to survive.

A stroke is a brain injury caused by lack of blood flow to the brain. It can happen if a blood vessel in the brain becomes clogged and blocks blood flow, or if a blood vessel ruptures and "bleeds out," leaking blood into the surrounding brain tissue. In both cases, oxygen-carrying blood doesn't get to where it needs to go in the brain.

Just like the heart, the brain needs oxygen to function. If the brain's blood flow is disrupted or blocked, the brain

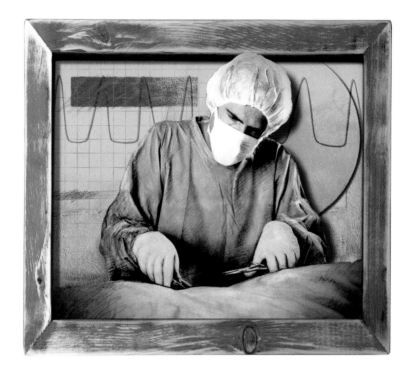

Smokers are more likely to need open-heart surgery.

can be permanently damaged resulting in death or permanent disability.

The U.S. Department of Health and Human Services estimates that smokers who smoke more than twenty-five cigarettes per day run the highest risk of developing a stroke. Why? Just as the chemicals in tobacco can constrict vessels that carry blood to the heart, they can constrict the vessels that carry blood to the brain. And just as smoking contributes to blood clots forming in coronary arteries, it can cause blood to clot in other parts of the body, including the brain.

Clearing the Haze

The heart and brain aren't the only parts of the body that can be damaged by tobacco use. The lungs can be, too (and not just from cancer).

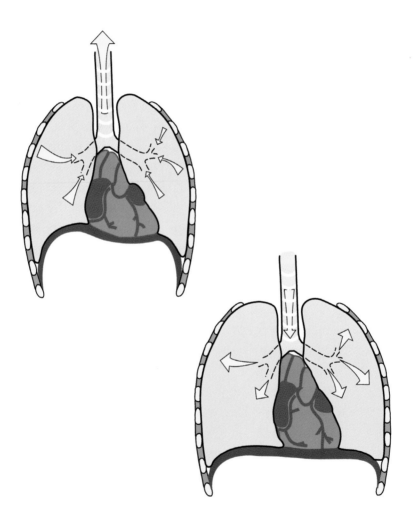

Tobacco and Chronic Lung Disorders

Amanda, Scott, Jolene, and Angel illustrate what can happen when tobacco use results in lung disease for smokers and nonsmokers alike. Most people are well aware that smoking cigarettes causes lung cancer, but smoking can also cause other, lifelong, debilitating lung disorders.

Two Kinds of Smoking

Active smoking is when a person puffs on a cigarette, bidi, cigar, or pipe—these are smokers. Passive smoking occurs when a person inhales someone else's tobacco smoke—these are nonsmokers. Inhaling secondhand smoke is so serious to your health it is considered passive smoking!

Chronic Bronchitis

Jolene wasn't even a smoker, yet she ended up with chronic bronchitis. How?

We learned in the previous chapter that air gets into our lungs by traveling down the windpipe into the bronchi, which connect the windpipe to the lungs. (The bronchi are sometimes also called the bronchial tubes.) Bronchitis is an inflammation of the lining of the bronchial tubes. When the bronchi are inflamed and/or infected, they produce a thick, cloudy mucous, called phlegm, and less air can flow through the tubes to and from the lungs. A person with bronchitis coughs hard

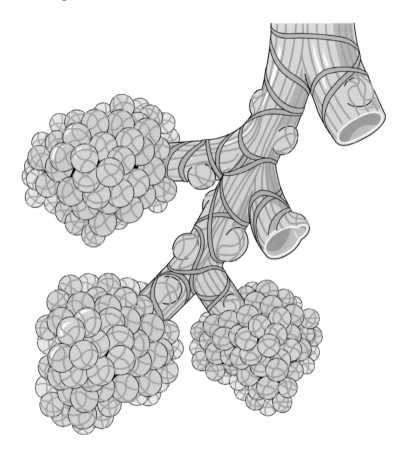

The alveoli are the tiny air sacs in the lungs. They can be damaged or even destroyed by tobacco smoke.

and coughs a lot, often coughing up the mucous, in an attempt to clear the airway. This kind of cough is commonly known as a "smoker's cough."

Jolene, though a nonsmoker herself, lived with a smoking family. The secondhand smoke she inhaled daily in her home chronically irritated her bronchial tubes. Because she could never get away from secondhand smoke, her bronchi were constantly inflamed. Her smoking family's choice to use tobacco cost Jolene the opportunity to have healthy lungs. The result was chronic bronchitis.

The American Lung Association states that smoking is the number-one cause of chronic bronchitis. People who smoke cigarettes are most likely to develop the disease, but those who inhale secondhand smoke can get it as well, just as Jolene did.

Chronic bronchitis can be treated. Most treatments for chronic bronchitis focus on reducing the inflammation of the bronchi. Sometimes, if a bacterial infection is present, antibacterial drugs will be used (called antibiotics). Treatment can also include the use of special inhalers whose medicines help the bronchi to open up more. One of the best treatment strategies is to reduce the source of irritation: if it's cigarette smoke, quit smoking. If it's secondhand smoke, move into a smoke-free environment or convince those around you to quit smoking.

Emphysema

Another chronic (long-lasting) lung disorder than can be caused by smoking is a condition called emphysema. In this case, the tiny air sacs in the lungs (called alveoli) become over-inflated, and as the disease progresses, they are destroyed. If you recall from the last chapter, the alveoli are where our bodies get rid of waste gasses, like carbon dioxide, and where they take in oxygen from the air. As the tiny air sacs are destroyed, it becomes more difficult for the lungs to get needed oxygen into the bloodstream, which causes shortness of breath. The earliest symptoms of emphysema are breathlessness during physical activity (like walking or going up steps) and coughing.

Though some forms of emphysema are inherited, smoking contributes to emphysema. In fact, according to the American Lung Association, smoking tobacco products causes more than 80 percent of emphysema cases. Unfortunately, this disease has no cure. Doctors can only make a person with emphysema live more comfortably with his disease while they try to slow down its progress.

The first advice doctors give patients with emphysema is this: "Quit smoking." Beyond that, inhalers, breathing exercises, and some surgeries are about all doctors can do.

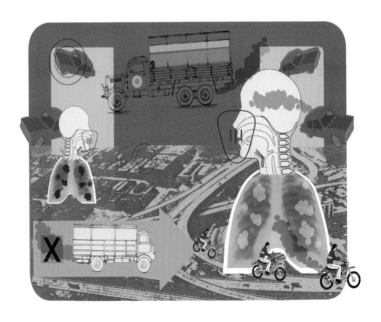

Air pollution can cause some of the same health problems as smoking does.

COPD:
Chronic
Obstructive
Pulmonary
Disease

Common Side Effects
of Smoking in Teens

Before teens develop chronic or life threatening diseases from smoking, they will experience other, less dramatic health effects:

- chronic, irritating coughs
- more frequent common colds
- longer lasting colds
- bronchitis or pneumonia
- greater susceptibility to the flu
- reduced stamina in sports
- sexual difficulty (impotence)

Though none of the teens who started this chapter had a chronic obstructive pulmonary disease (COPD), a few were well on their way. COPD is the name given to a group of lung diseases that block airflow into the lungs and that occur simultaneously. When a person has chronic bronchitis and emphysema together, for example, she is said to have COPD. This disease usually includes some combination of emphysema, chronic bronchitis, and asthma.

COPD is the fourth leading cause of death in the United States and Canada, and a leading cause of illness and disability in the United States. The CDC estimates that over ten million adults were diagnosed with COPD in the United States in 2000 alone; if you take COPD

Kicking the habit may be difficult—but the health benefits are worth it.

death rates into account, over twenty-four million Americans currently have the condition.

Tobacco use is the primary cause of COPD, but asthma, air pollution, ***genetic*** factors, and respiratory infections can also play a role. The CDC identifies avoidance of tobacco smoke and air pollutants as a primary means of treatment of COPD. Like emphysema, this condition has no cure.

As we've seen in this chapter and the previous chapter, teens who smoke put themselves at great risk for developing big, bad, ugly conditions like various cancers, heart disease, stroke, and lung conditions. Most of these

Even Tobacco Company People Aren't Immune

These tobacco company personnel have experienced or died from tobacco-related diseases:

- R. J. Reynolds (founder of R.J. Reynolds Tobacco Co.), died of emphysema at age 58
- R. J. Reynolds III (grandson of R.J. above), died of emphysema at age 60
- Wayne McLaren (a Marlboro model), died of lung cancer at age 51
- David Miller (the original Marlboro man), died of emphysema
- David Goerlitz (the Winston man), disabled by a stroke in his mid-thirties
- Will Thornbury (Camel model), died of lung cancer at age 56
- Janet Sackman (Lucky Strike girl), had cancer of the larynx and lungs

conditions, however, take years to develop. The effects of tobacco use, unless seen firsthand in a dying loved one, are usually not enough to ***deter*** teens from smoking; the consequences are simply too far away.

But smoking has other, more immediate side effects teens should consider.

5

Bad Breath, Teeth Troubles, Smelly Shirts, and Disappearing Dollars

Josh, at eighteen, can legally buy cigarettes in his state. As a moderate smoker, he only goes through about two packs of cigarettes per week. At five dollars per pack, he really doesn't think it's costing him that much money—ten bucks per week. Ten dollars a week for fifty-two weeks adds up to only $520 a year. That doesn't seem like much money. It's not that expensive.

But what about over his entire lifetime? Let's say that Josh is one of the lucky few smokers who doesn't die prematurely from tobacco-related illnesses. Let's assume that he lives to be seventy-eight years old. That measly $520 per year adds up to $31,200 for the sixty years he lives beyond the age of eighteen. If Josh thought about it, he could probably come up with a long list of things he'd rather buy for $31,200 than 6,240 packages of cigarettes.

Now, let's imagine that Josh isn't a moderate smoker, but a heavy smoker instead. Rather than two packs of cigarettes a week, he goes through two packs of cigarettes per *day* (a common amount for heavy smokers). His financial costs have now skyrocketed! Ten dollars per day for a week is seventy dollars; for a whole year it adds up

to $3,650. Over sixty years, it cost him $219,000! Imagine what he could buy with that if he wasn't a smoker. That much money is a lot to invest in something that will kill you.

Smoking Costs Something

No matter how you look at it, smoking costs something. At the very least, as we saw with Josh, it costs money— money that could otherwise be spent on CDs, DVDs, stereo systems, computer equipment, clothing, sports events, books, movie tickets, gasoline for the car, snacks, eating out, hobby supplies, or just about anything. You can't spend the same dollar twice: money spent on cigarettes is gone for good; you can't get it back again.

Of course, money isn't the only cost involved in tobacco use. We've seen in earlier chapters that smoking can cost you your health and even your life. Yet there are still more costs than these.

How Smoking Affects Your Appearance

Smoking can give you:

- dry skin
- yellow teeth
- bleeding gums
- stained fingers
- stringy hair
- wrinkled skin

APPEARANCE

Many teens only look at the white cylinder hanging out of the sexy movie star's lips when they think about smoking and appearance. Tobacco advertisers would have us believe their image. What many tobacco users don't realize is that smoking and chewing tobacco can damage a person's physical appearance.

The tar in tobacco smoke leaves a yellowish-brown coating on the teeth and skin. That's why so many smokers have yellow-tinted teeth and fingertips. Short-term use of chewing tobacco can cause cracked lips and bleeding in the mouth. Smoking can strip oils out of the skin, leaving it dry, leathery, and deeply wrinkled. Over time, smoking can also lead to tooth loss. The Academy of General Dentistry reports that a one-pack-a-day smoking habit can cost the loss of at least two teeth every ten years. In addition, research shows that smokers experience more gum disease than nonsmokers, which contributes to even more tooth loss. Smokers even lose more hair than nonsmokers, and what hair they keep is often dry and brittle.

Think about it: how many yellow-finger-stained, toothless, balding, wrinkle-faced actresses with cigarettes hanging out of cracked bleeding lips do you see in tobacco advertisements? None. That's because tobacco companies want you to think that smoking will make you physically attractive, when in fact, the opposite is true. Smoking robs you of youth and beauty.

Smoking doesn't just hurt your looks, though; it can hurt your relationships, too.

Bad Breath ... Disappearing Dollars

SOCIAL COSTS

Would you agree or disagree with the following statements?

Seeing someone smoke turns me off.
I'd rather date people who don't smoke.
I strongly dislike being around smokers.

These statements appeared on a recent survey done by the CDC to study teen opinions on smoking. How did teens across America respond to the same three statements? Sixty-seven percent said that seeing someone smoke turned them off; 86 percent said they'd rather date people who didn't smoke; and 65 percent said they strongly disliked being around smokers! Clearly, smoking is not the "in" thing to do these days. In fact, far more teens do *not* smoke than do. Smoking just isn't as cool as it used to be.

Smoking can be more isolating than you think, and not just because of other teens' opinions: ducking out of concerts or sports events to grab a quick smoke; going outside for a cigarette to avoid stinking up the house; having to leave a nonsmoking restaurant to get a nicotine fix—these actions pull you away from the daily activities of life. They keep you from participating in things the way nonsmokers do. They can also cost you potential relationships.

Think of the girl who nags her boyfriend to quit smoking, but he won't. More than a few teens have bailed on relationships because their partners refused to quit. Or what about the nonsmoking guy who likes a girl but won't ask her out because of her habit? Think of what might have been if only she'd dumped nicotine.

Clearing the Haze

Bad Breath ... Disappearing Dollars

In the United States, in most states, it's illegal to buy, sell, or have tobacco products in your possession if you're less than eighteen years of age. Smoking in school or having tobacco products in your possession can get you bounced from your sports team and suspended from class—even more isolation.

Smoking has many social costs. It's even been linked to high-risk behaviors like having unprotected sex or experimenting with drugs. The CDC estimates that teens who smoke are three times more likely to use alcohol than nonsmokers, eight times more likely to use marijuana, and twenty-two times more likely to use cocaine.

> **Did You Know?**
>
> Most nonsmoking teenagers say they would *not* consider dating someone who smoked. They find smoking unattractive.

One less tangible social cost is image. Though hard to define, image is that appearance we give to people around us—to peers, family, coworkers, coaches, teachers, employers—with the hopes that they'll like or approve of us. Let's face it: deep down we want other people to like us. We like to impress people. Smoking, however, does little to impress; it is often seen as a ***detriment*** instead. Many people, especially adults, see teen smokers as troublemakers or outcasts, not as confident capable young men and women. Smoking doesn't create a positive impression. It doesn't even offer a neutral impression. If anything, smoking leaves a negative impression.

That's what Sam found out.

Clearing the Haze

Sam and Toni each interviewed to work at a local family restaurant. It was a part-time job clearing tables for just above minimum wage. Both were sixteen years old; both could drive and had dependable cars; both got good grades; both were involved in sports and other activities in school; both had solid recommendations; and for both, this would be a first job. When each interviewed with the prospective employer, both were polite, made good eye contact, and answered questions well. The only difference in their applications was that Sam smoked. Toni got the job. Why? Because the fact that Toni was a nonsmoker made a better first impression.

Whether it's fair or not, whether it's right or not, whether it's even an accurate perception or not, the reality is many people respect those who choose *not* to smoke more than they respect those who do. That's just the way it is.

"I don't care what other people think of me," you might argue. That may well be true. But you probably care very much about whether you can run without wheezing or walk up a flight of stairs.

Fitness

One teenager's experience described in an article published jointly by the National Institute on Drug Abuse (NIDA) and Scholastic, Inc., captures the impact smoking can have on teen fitness. Kevin McNamara, an eighteen-year-old high school senior and one of the teens interviewed for the article, was a star member of his school's golf team and the best pitcher on the baseball

Clearing the Haze

Smoking can interfere with fitness.

Question: I know smoking a lot can make me sick, but what if I only smoke a little? Is that safe?

Answer: No, smoking a little is still not safe. There is no "safe" amount of smoking, just as there is no "safe" cigarette. Every puff takes in toxins from tobacco smoke, and causes some harm, no matter how small.

team until he tore a ligament in his knee. The young athlete also smoked two packs of cigarettes a day.

"I used to be able to run a mile in under six minutes," Kevin says in the article. "Now I'm lucky to make it in eight. And I'm wheezing all the way."

Because smoking interferes with the body's ability to take oxygen in through the lungs, it's harder for the lungs to keep up with the demands the body makes for oxygen during exercise. Teen athletes who smoke see their ath-

Other Things Tobacco Can Do to You

Smoking or chewing tobacco can . . .

- make you smell like an ashtray.
- make you wheeze when you breathe.
- give you sores in your mouth.
- deaden your senses of smell and taste.
- make your eyes itch and water.
- rot your gums.
- make you get more colds and flus.

letic performances slip: they can't practice as hard as they once did or run as long; they have reduced **stamina** and muscle strength. They find themselves panting and wheezing over what used to be easy-to-accomplish fitness goals. Their conditioning falters because the body can't get the oxygen it needs—all because of smoking.

Kevin's reduced fitness made him ready to give up smoking. By the time of the article's printing, Kevin had cut his habit back from two packs a day to ten cigarettes a day, and counting. "I want to quit," he says toward the end of the interview, "but it's not that easy." Maybe by now Kevin is smoke-free.

EMOTIONAL COSTS

Many teens start smoking for emotional reasons: wanting to be accepted or included by friends; not wanting to feel insecure; looking for thrills or excitement; fearing ridicule or exclusion; wanting to look mature, and a host of other reasons. But once you're hooked on tobacco, another set of emotional costs comes into play. Nineteen-year-old Darlene explains how this played out in her early teen years.

I first tried cigarettes when a bunch of kids from my church's youth group were hanging outside the gymnasium after a volleyball tournament. I was thirteen and a few of the older kids, some senior high kids, had cigarettes they'd stolen from their parents, so I took a few drags off of theirs. I really wanted to be liked, and smoking with them made me feel like a part of their group. I found out later that they weren't really my friends; they just wanted to see

me get into trouble. By the time I realized that it didn't matter; I was already hooked.

I started stealing cigarettes from my grandmother who lived with us. She had one of these old-fashioned cigarette cases, the kind that squeezes shut at the top, and I could sneak one or two cigarettes out at a time without her noticing. When my parents' smelled tobacco smoke on my clothes and hair and asked me about it, I lied. I told them one of my friends had been smoking, or that I'd been sitting with my grandmother while she smoked.

Peer pressure often plays a major role in the decision to smoke.

That kind of lie turned into even bigger lies, and I felt worse and worse with each lie I told. Up until then, my mom, dad, and I got along okay, but lying was eating me up inside. I started to get cranky and defensive over stupid

97

things. I avoided them, and when I couldn't avoid them, I blew up at them. I slammed doors. I yelled. I fought. I was so angry. But I wasn't really angry at them. I was mad at me.

I just felt so guilty. And I was disappointed, mostly in myself. So I promised myself I'd stop. I'd stop the lies, I'd stop the smoking, and I'd stop the deceit.

*Stopping wasn't as easy as I thought it would be. When I went a whole day without a cigarette I felt nervous and crabby. I was constantly on edge—snapping at everybody just like I had been before. I didn't know then that my feelings were a normal part of nicotine **withdrawal**—it was how my body reacted to wanting but not getting more nicotine. So I felt guilty some more. Fighting with everyone, hating myself, hating that I ever started smoking, but hating that I had to stop—I thought I was losing my mind.*

Darlene's experience is pretty common to teen smokers. And it illustrates how smoking can takes its toll emotionally, anywhere from the lies it takes to get cigarettes when you're underage to the emotional turmoil quitting can cause as your body craves nicotine.

Sure, smoking might provide a momentary sense of pleasure. But is that sporadic minute of pleasure worth hours, days, weeks, or months of pain?

Smoking costs a bunch, doesn't it? To be a smoker, you have to be willing to pay. Are you willing to pay the finan-

---

Sobering Statistics

Despite drug awareness education efforts, more teenage girls—30 percent more, to be exact—are smoking now than smoked ten years ago.

cial costs? Are you willing to sacrifice your appearance? Are you willing to go through the isolation and rejection that comes with smoking? Are you willing to trade in your fitness and reputation? Are you willing to pay the emotional costs of smoking, and later of quitting, should you choose to smoke? These are just some of the immediate costs; the costs you experience here and now, today. Let's not forget the costs discussed in earlier chapters. Is smoking really worth your health and life?

Only you can decide.

6
Is It Worth It?

You Decide

SCENARIO ONE: You're a fourteen-year-old high school freshman. You have a crush on a senior who's on the swim team with you, but you don't say anything to him because you're afraid he might think you're just a kid. At a post swim-meet party, you see him smoking and wonder if he'll think you're more mature if you light up, too. You've never smoked before. What would you do?

SCENARIO TWO: You're fifteen. Your parents smoke. Your older brothers smoke. Their friends all smoke. At a New Year's Eve party when everyone is at your house, your nineteen-year-old brother hands you a cigarette in front of his friends, and says to you, "C'mon, stop bein' a kid. When are you gonna grow up and be a man?" What would you do?

SCENARIO THREE: You just got paid for your babysitting job, and you've been saving up for a new CD player. You don't have that much more to go until you can afford the CD player you've been hoping to get. Your best friend, however, decides she wants to experiment with smoking and asks you to split the cost of a carton of cigarettes. What will you do?

SCENARIO FOUR: You just passed your driver's test, and your grandparents have offered to give you their late-model used car to have as your own, but only if you're willing to pay for your own car insurance. You're also a smoker with a two-pack-a-day habit. You know you can't afford both. Which will you choose?

SCENARIO FIVE: You've been going out with this really cute, athletic guy for the last three months. He's a nice guy—polite and sensitive, and you really like him. But you just found out that he uses chewing tobacco. You think it's gross, and can't stand to watch him spit, but you think he's cool anyway. There's just one problem: the thought of kissing him now gives you really mixed feel-ings. You're excited about kissing him but hate the

Growing up means you'll need to make decisions about many areas of your life.

thought of what's been in his mouth. In addition, you know that chewing tobacco can be really bad for his health, and you're worried about him. You're afraid to say anything, however, because you think he'll dump you. What will you do?

Real life. Real teens. Real situations. Only you can decide what you would do in each scenario. The best way to handle situations like these, however, is to weigh the costs and benefits ahead of time and decide what you would do *before* you're actually faced with the situation. Hopefully, this book will allow you to do just that.

The main purpose of this book is to give you enough factual information about tobacco use and its hazards and pleasures to make an informed, responsible choice about smoking. Choosing to smoke is an expensive proposition. Can you afford to make that decision?

> *"There's hard evidence that smoking leads to addiction, health problems, and death. . . . Teens have a choice: They can become victims, or they can stop before they go too far. Better yet, they never have to start at all."*
>
> —Dr. Eric Moolchan, director of NIDA's Teen Tobacco Addiction Treatment Research Clinic

Perhaps you've decided that smoking isn't for you. Congratulations! You've made one of the best choices you can make for your long-term health. Not everyone will support your decision and you will need courage to stand by your ***convictions***, but you can gain confidence

> ### Did You Know?
>
> Girls between the ages of twelve and nineteen years old are more likely to try to quit smoking than boys of that age.

from knowing that you studied the facts and made a deliberate choice. It's a choice you're likely to revisit as your life and circumstances change. You can be sure with every decision you make to resist smoking, you'll grow more confident in the soundness of the choice for you.

But what if you're already smoking? What if you're already addicted to nicotine? What if after learning the facts about tobacco's effects you realize that you really don't want to smoke after all? It's not too late. You can choose to stop, and stop successfully, if you know how and where to get the help you need.

If You're Ready to Quit

If you're thinking about giving up tobacco, you're not alone. A study done in July of 2003 by the American Legacy Foundation (an independent public health foundation created as a result of a 1998 tobacco settlement) found that over two-thirds of young women smokers aged sixteen to twenty-three wanted to quit smoking and were thinking about trying to quit within the next six months. Over a quarter of young men who smoked wanted to do the same. But be prepared: wanting doesn't always mean doing. And quitting, if you choose to do so, won't be easy.

Hurdle #1:
Nicotine Withdrawal

We saw in earlier chapters that nicotine is a highly addictive chemical found in tobacco, and that when smoke is inhaled, nicotine is carried to the lungs, then into the bloodstream, and to the brain where it affects chemical neurotransmitters. Nicotine actually changes your brain's chemical makeup. As you get used to having nicotine in your body, you tend to need more of the drug to satisfy your cravings for it, until your body adapts to a

Is It Worth It? You Decide

Question: Why is quitting smoking so hard?

Answer: Quitting is difficult because nicotine dependence involves both the mind and the body. It is a physical and psychological addiction.

higher level of nicotine in your blood and brain. In other words, your body gets used to having nicotine in its system and adapts. Then it wants more.

When you suddenly take nicotine away, your body craves it, making you feel like you need to have more nicotine or you'll die or get sick or something drastic will happen. When that craving is frustrated, your body rebels with all kinds of symptoms: headaches, fatigue, trouble sleeping, trouble paying attention, irritability, feelings of anger and frustration, anxiety, depression, hunger, thirst, agitation, and the jitters. These symptoms can be quite severe, and can appear in just a few short hours after your last cigarette. They will be at their worst two to three days later if you don't smoke at all during that time, and can last for weeks. Sometimes withdrawal symptoms are so bad, people feel like they have no choice but to smoke to ease their discomfort. This is why so many people try to quit and fail.

This immediate and complete removal of nicotine from smokers is called quitting "cold turkey." It means choosing to stop, and never smoking again without any help or intervention. While admirable, this approach will work for only

According to the CDC, fewer than one in ten people who try to quit smoking actually succeed in doing so the first time. Yet, over fifty million Americans are former smokers.

some people. Because nicotine is such a powerful substance, others might need to be tapered off it slowly—they need help.

Slowly reducing the number of cigarettes you smoke in a day can be a means of tapering off, but the many nicotine replacement products available on the market today make that unnecessary.

NICOTINE REPLACEMENTS

The idea behind nicotine replacement products is that they can give you a small dose of nicotine (a "fix") periodically once you quit smoking to help reduce your body's craving for nicotine without a need to smoke. These products only deal with the physical addiction to nicotine, not the psychological.

Many types of nicotine substitute products are available to help you quit smoking:

- nicotine patch (provides measured nicotine doses through a small patch worn on the skin over longer periods of time)
- nicotine gum (more immediate acting, this chewing gum provides a dose of nicotine through the membranes of the mouth)
- nicotine nasal spray (available only with a prescription from your doctor, this spray delivers a direct dose of nicotine through the lining of the nose)
- nicotine inhalers (availably only with a prescription from your doctor, this inhaler delivers nicotine vapors to the mouth when you puff on it)
- nicotine lozenges (a small hard candy-like drop that you suck on until it dissolves)

Other products, like nicotine lollipops, nicotine lip balms, and tobacco lozenges have not been reviewed or approved by the **U.S. Food and Drug Administration**, and are not considered "safe" to use. They can be especially dangerous for young children.

Sometimes, nicotine replacements don't work. In these cases, your doctor may prescribe certain medications to use with nicotine replacement strategies or to use on their own. Keep in mind that nicotine replacements or pills from your doctor may not be all you need to quit. Most people need some kind of emotional or relational support, too.

Hurdle #2: Psychological Dependence

Smokers don't just depend on nicotine physically. They depend on it behaviorally and psychologically. Smoking can be the thing you do when you get together with friends. It may be your means to blow off steam when you feel tense. Lighting up may be part of your family culture or religious *ideals*. Quitting means that all those things will have to change in some way, at least for you. It's not easy.

One way to make the transition easier is to be prepared. Set a date for when you'll quit. Throw out all your tobacco products. Let a friend know that you're attempting to quit starting on your specified date. Then think through how you plan to deal with the times you're tempted to smoke.

How will you handle your urges to put something in your mouth, for example? Try gum, hard candy, lollipops, crunchy raw vegetables, nuts, or flavored tooth-picks. What about when you're angry? Maybe rather than lighting up, you can go for a run instead. The idea is to *replace* the former behavior with a new, different, healthier-for-you behavior.

Some people find that something as simple as chewing ice cubes can help them kick the smoking habit.

Here's another example. If you know that you're tempted to smoke when you're bored, plan to be extremely busy for the first few days after you quit: get together with nonsmoking friends, go shopping, work extra hours, do hand crafts, play a musical instrument, have a video-game marathon, take in a double feature at the movie theater, go to the local gym, add an extra workout, go out of town, take a camping trip. Again, replace the smoking behavior with something new and pleasurable.

Five Keys for Quitting

1. Get ready.
2. Get support.
3. Learn new skills and behaviors.
4. Get medication and use it correctly.
5. Be prepared for relapse or difficult situations.

Use all five together for the best chances of successful quitting.

(Recommended by the U.S. Dept. of Health and Human Services.)

Try changing your routine or doing something you haven't done before. Take a class at the public library or local YMCA. Join a fitness club. Investigate a new committee or team at school. Volunteer at your local hospital or library (you can't smoke at either of these places). Get a different part-time job. The excitement and newness of the change will keep you from becoming bored and restless.

Clearing the Haze

If you know that a certain circle of friends pressures you to smoke, make arrangements to hang out with different, nonsmoking friends for the first two weeks after you quit. Then practice how you'll handle your smoking friends before you put yourself in that situation.

Hurdle #3: Maintaining Your Change

Many former smokers are able to quit for one day or one week or even one month. But becoming permanently nicotine-free requires work and diligence. Here are a few strategies that might help for the long haul (adapted from the American Cancer Society's Guide for Quitting Smoking):

1. Try positive self-talk. Tell yourself the truth. When the cravings are at their worst, remind yourself that even though they feel overwhelming right now, they won't last forever. The craving will pass. That's true.
2. Recognize false self-talk, also called "rationalization." Thoughts like *If I don't smoke, I can't have fun* or *one little cigarette won't hurt, will it?* are simply not true. Recognize them for the lies or false beliefs they are, and then abandon them.
3. Avoid situations where you are most tempted to smoke. You know best what these may be. Maybe it's a certain group of friends or school activity or hang out. Stay away from

these until you're sure you can handle them without smoking.

4. Take up exercise, if you don't exercise regularly already. It will keep you busy, tire you out, reduce your stress, help you sleep, and distract you.

5. Drink lots of water or juice, and avoid sugared drinks and caffeinated beverages.

6. Set short-term, manageable goals. If your cravings for tobacco are particularly strong, tell yourself, *I'll wait ten minutes; I can hang in there for ten more minutes.* Then when those ten minutes are up, try again. This technique is called "delay." By delaying your gratification for a few moments, it is often enough to get you through until the craving passes.

7. Remember, for the former smoker, there is NO SUCH THING AS JUST ONE MORE PUFF or JUST ONE MORE CIGARETTE. Addiction doesn't work that way.

8. Find a trusted friend or two that you can call for support when your cravings are at their worst.

9. Expect to have bad days (when you feel depressed or lethargic) and to experience some downsides to quitting (like mild weight gain). These are normal, and are NOT failures. But if they get the best of you and you end up blowing it, just dust yourself off and try again. Don't ever quit on quitting.

10. Write down all your reasons for going tobacco-free and keep them in a place where you can remind yourself of them often. Need some ideas? Here are just a few.

Clearing the Haze

As a young adult, you need to make decisions that are good for you, both now and in the future.

Benefits of Quitting

Of course every individual has his or her own reasons for quitting smoking. Some quit because they're afraid of tobacco's long-term health effects on the body or because they want to improve their physical fitness. Others quit because they're tired of coughing and smelling like cigarette smoke all the time. Still others quit because they don't want to waste the money or they want loved ones to quit harassing them about smoking. The most tragic cases are those who quit because using tobacco has already given them a fatal disease. Yet virtually all people who try to "kick the habit" do so because they want to feel better.

Amazingly, quitting can have almost immediate beneficial effects. Consider these benefits of quitting provided by the American Lung Association:

- **Twenty minutes after quitting:** blood pressure decreases; pulse rate drops; body temperature of hands and feet increases.
- **Eight hours after quitting:** carbon monoxide level in blood drops to normal; oxygen level in blood increases to normal.
- **Twenty-four hours after quitting:** chance of a heart attack decreases.
- **Forty-eight hours after quitting:** nerve endings start to regrow; ability to smell and taste is enhanced.
- **From two weeks to three months after quitting:** circulation improves; walking becomes easier; lung function increases.
- **From one month to nine months after quitting:** coughing, sinus congestion, fatigue, shortness of breath decreases.

115

- **One year after quitting:** excess risk of coronary heart disease is decreased to half that of a smoker.
- **From five to fifteen years after quitting:** stroke risk is reduced to that of people who have never smoked.
- **Ten years after quitting:** risk of lung cancer drops to as little as one-half that of continuing smokers; risk of cancer of the mouth, throat, esophagus, bladder, kidney, and pancreas decreases; risk of ulcer decreases.
- **Fifteen years after quitting:** risk of coronary heart disease is now similar to that of people who have never smoked; risk of death returns to nearly the level of people who have never smoked.

Almost Immediate Benefits of Quitting

- better breath
- more spending money
- better smelling hair and clothes
- improved sense of taste and smell
- greater self-confidence

Regardless of your reason for choosing to quit, know this: you *can* do it. And by taking the steps to quit you're doing something terrific not only for yourself but for your loved ones. As you move forward in this journey of recovery from nicotine addiction, take time to reward yourself. Use some of that money you would have spent on cigarettes or chew to treat yourself to other things. Celebrate your ***milestones***: one day smoke-free; one week smoke-free; one month smoke-free; three months smoke-free, and so on. Every day you get through without choosing to use tobacco moves you closer to better health—one day, one choice at a time.

Consider this day the first day of the rest of your life.

FURTHER READING

Dodd, Bill. *1440 Reasons to Quit Smoking: One for Every Minute of the Day.* Minnetonka, Minn.: Meadowbrook, 2000.

Ferguson, Tom. *No-Nag, No-Guilt, Do-It-Your-Own-Way Guide to Quitting Smoking.* New York: Ballantine Books, 1998.

Fisher, Edwin B. *The American Lung Association 7 Steps to a Smoke-Free Life.* Hoboken, N.J.: John Wiley & Sons, 1998.

Hepburn, Susan. *Stop Smoking in One Hour: Play the CD . . . Just Once . . . And Never Smoke Again.* London, U.K.: Thorsons, 2001.

Klienman, Lowell, et al. *The Complete Idiot's Guide to Quitting Smoking.* Indianapolis, Ind.: Alpha Books, 2000.

Kranz, Rachel. *Straight Talk About Smoking.* New York: Facts on File, 1999.

Lang, Susan and Beth Marks. *Teens and Tobacco: A Fatal Attraction.* New York: Twenty-First Century Books, 1996.

Moe, Barbara. *Teen Smoking and Tobacco Use: A Hot Topic.* Berkeley Heights, N.J.: Enslow, 2000.

Pietrusza, David. *Smoking.* San Diego, Calif.: Lucent, 1997.

Action on Smoking and Health (ASH)
2013 H Street, N.W.
Washington, DC 20006, USA
(202) 659-4310
ash.org/kids.html

American Cancer Society (ACS)
(800) ACS-2345
www.cancer.org

American Heart Association (AHA)
National Center
7272 Greenville Avenue
Dallas, TX 75231
(800) AHA-USA-1 (800) 242-8721
www.americanheart.org

American Lung Association
The American Lung Association
61 Broadway, 6th Floor
New York, NY 10006
(212) 315-8700
www.lungusa.org

BAD Advertising Institute
c/o Xiamen University, Xiamen, China
International Telephone: 86 (592) 218-2565
(China is 12 hours ahead of EST)
U.S. Telephone: (908) 273-9368 (c/o NJ GASP)
U.S. Mailing Address:
c/o NJ GASP
105 Mountain Ave
Summit, NJ 07901
www.badvertising.org

GASP Magazine (on-line downloadable version)
www.tobaccofacts.org/pdf/gasp2001.pdf

National Center for Chronic Disease Prevention Office
on Smoking & Health
National Center for Chronic Disease Prevention
Centers for Disease Control and Prevention
U.S. Department of Health & Human Services
200 Independence Avenue, S.W.
Washington, D.C. 20201
www.cdc.gov/tobacco

National Institute on Drug Abuse (NIDA)
6001 Executive Blvd.
Bethesda, MD 20892-9561
(301) 443-1124
www.drugabuse.gov

Nicotine Addiction and Other Dangers of Tobacco Use
A Service of the National Institute of Drug Abuse
(NIDA)
smoking.drugabuse.gov

Nicotine Free Kids
www.nicotinefreekids.com

NIDA for Teens
teens.drugabuse.gov

SGR for Kids (The Surgeon General's Report for Kids
About Smoking)
www.cdc.gov/tobacco/sgr/sgr4kids/realdeal.htm

TeenQuit.com
www.teenquit.com

The Truth
www.thetruth.com

TIPS for Youth
Tobacco Information and Prevention Source (TIPS)
National Center for Chronic Disease Prevention
Centers for Disease Control and Prevention
U.S. Department of Health & Human Services
200 Independence Avenue, S.W.
Washington, D.C. 20201
www.cdc.gov/tobacco/tips4youth.htm

Publisher's note:
The Web sites listed on these pages were active at the time of publication. The publisher is not responsible for Web sites that have changed their addresses or discontinued operation since the date of publication. The publisher will review and update the Web sites upon each reprint.

anxiety disorders Psychological disorders that involve painful or apprehensive uneasiness of mind.

asthma A condition often of allergic origin that is marked by continuous labored breathing accompanied by wheezing, by a sense of constriction in the chest, and often by attacks of coughing or gasping.

blatantly Conspicuously; obviously.

bombarded Persistently assailed.

bronchitis (bron-KITE-is) Acute or chronic inflammation of the bronchial tubes; also a disease marked by this.

convictions Strong beliefs.

deter To discourage or prevent from acting.

detriment Damage or injury.

DNA Any of several nucleic acids that are usually the molecular basis for heredity.

emphysema (em-fa-SEE-muh) A condition of the lung marked by abnormal dilation of its air spaces and distension of its walls and frequently by impairment of heart action.

enticements Things used to tempt or lure by arousing desire or hope.

euphoria (you-FOR-ee-uh) A feeling of well-being or elation.

genetic Relating to heredity.

guttural (GUT-er-ul) Uttered in the throat, often sounding strange or unpleasant.

ideals Standards of excellence, perfection, or beauty.

intracerebral hemorrhage Heavy or uncontrollable bleeding in the cerebrum—the part of the brain considered to be the base of conscious mental processes.

invincible Unable to be overcome, subdued, or

conquered.

leukemia (loo-KEE-mee-uh) A cancer that starts in the bone marrow and makes it hard to develop healthy blood cells.

mentholated Containing a crystalline alcohol (menthol) that occurs in mint leaves and has both the smell and cooling taste of peppermint.

milestones Significant points in development.

plague An epidemic of a virulent, contagious febrile (feverish) disease that causes high mortality.

plaque (plack) Injury to the inner walls of the arteries due to abnormal fatty deposits on the inner walls of the arteries.

psychoactive Affecting the mind or behavior.

seizures Sudden attacks of electrical activity within the brain, causing changes in consciousness and body movements.

squamous cell carcinoma (SQWOM-us cell CAR-si-noh-muh) An oral cancer that attacks cells in the compound bone of the side of the skull.

stamina Endurance; staying power.

stimulant An agent (as a drug) that produces a temporary increase of the functional activity or efficiency of an organism or any of its parts.

stunted Hindered the normal growth or progress of.

tethered Fastened to or restrained as if by a tether, a chain or rope used to limit an animal's range.

trachea (TRAY-kee-uh) The main base of the system of tubes allowing air to pass to and from the lungs in vertebrates.

upper respiratory failure Failure of the lungs to function properly, where either the level of oxygen in the blood becomes dangerously low, or the level of carbon dioxide becomes too high.

U.S. Food and Drug Administration A law enforcement agency in the United States that inspects,
tests, and sets standards for foodstuffs, medicines,
and medical devices, and is also involved with the
regulations governing associated products and lo-
cations that might affect personal health.

withdrawal The often physically and psychologically painful syndrome associated with discontinued use of an addictive substance.

INDEX

PICTURE CREDITS

Joan Esherick is a full-time author, freelance writer, and professional speaker who lives outside of Philadelphia, Pennsylvania, with her husband, three teenagers, and black Labrador retriever named Baxter. She is the author of ten books, including *Our Mighty Fortress: Finding Refuge in God* (Moody Press, 2002), *The Big Picture: The Bible's Story in Thirty Short Scenes*, and multiple books with Mason Crest Publishers. Joan has contributed dozens of articles to national print periodicals and speaks nationwide. For more information about her you can visit her web site at www.joanesherick.com.

Mary Ann McDonnell, APRN, BC, is an advanced practice nurse, the director of the clinical trials program in pediatric psychopharmacology research at Massachusetts General Hospital, has a private practice in pediatric psychopharmacology, and is a clinical instructor for Northeastern University and Boston College advanced practice nursing students. Her areas of expertise are bipolar disorder in children and adolescents, ADHD, and depression. Mary Ann is one of a small group of advanced practice nurses working in pediatric psychopharmacology research and practice who has a national reputation as an expert advanced practice nurse in the field of pediatric bipolar disorder, ADHD, and depression. She sits on the institutional review board and the research education committee at Massachusetts General Hospital and is a lecturer for local and national educational conferences on bipolar disorder, depression, and ADHD.

Dr. Sara Forman graduated from Barnard College and Harvard Medical School. She completed her residency in Pediatrics at Children's Hospital of Philadelphia and a fellowship in Adolescent Medicine at Children's Hospital Boston (CHB). She currently is an attending in Adolescent Medicine at CHB, where she has served as Director of the Adolescent Outpatient Eating Disorders Program for the past nine years. She has also consulted for the National Eating Disorder Screening Project on its high school initiative and has presented at many conferences about teens and eating disorders. In addition to her clinical and administrative roles in the Eating Disorders Program, Dr. Forman teaches medical students and residents and coordinates the Adolescent Medicine rotation at CHB. Dr. Forman sees primary care adolescent patients in the Adolescent Clinic at CHB, at Bentley College, and at the Germaine Lawrence School, a residential school for emotionally disturbed teenage girls.